The AB Papers

First Published 2019

Published in the United Kingdom
in 2019 by The QB Papers

Design by Burgess Studio
Printed on Munken Pure Rough Cream
Printed in the UK by Principal Colour
Typeset in Garamond

ISBN 978-1-913119-05-8

The Alternative Sports Olympics

Quentin Blake

The RB Papers

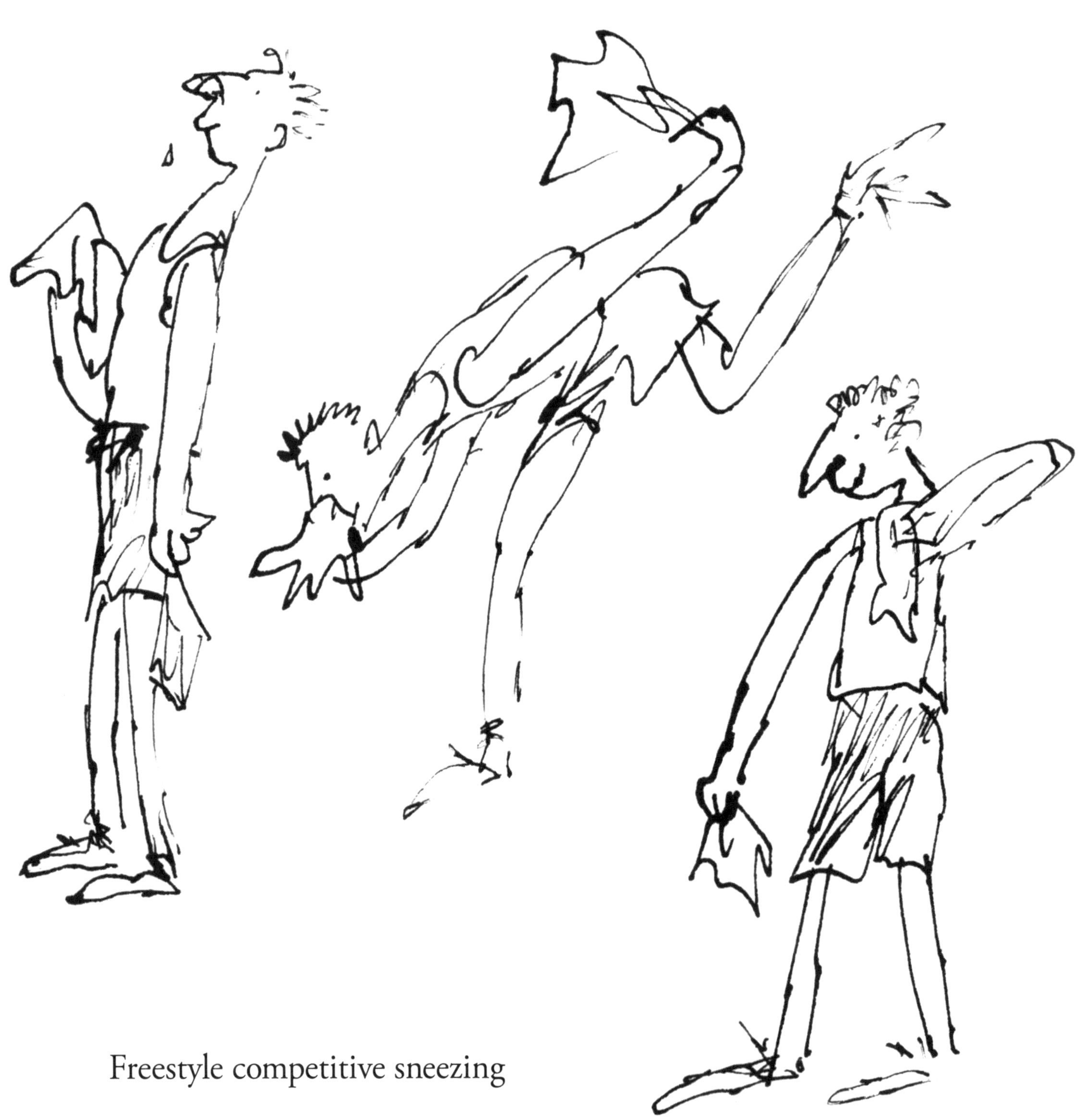

Freestyle competitive sneezing

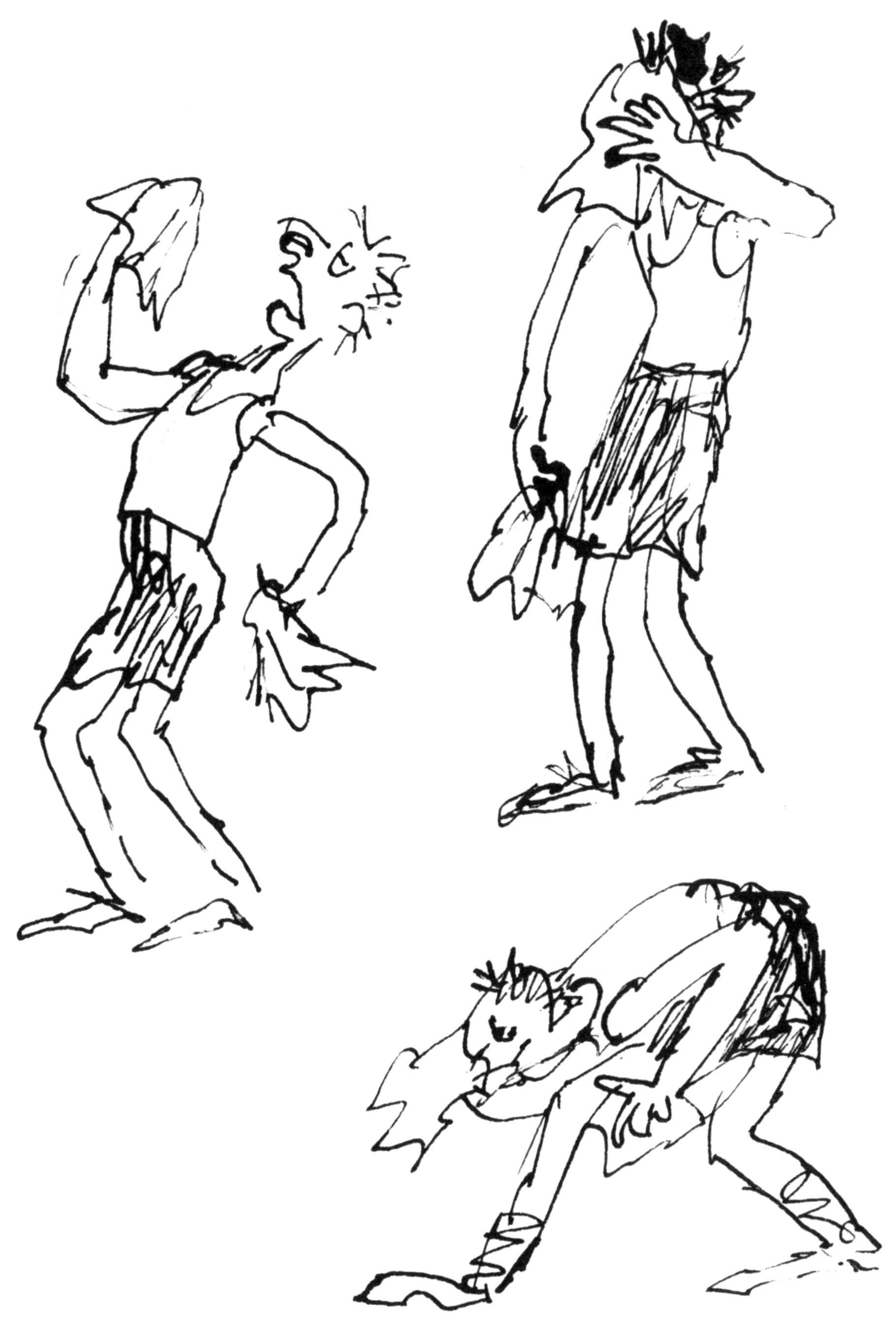

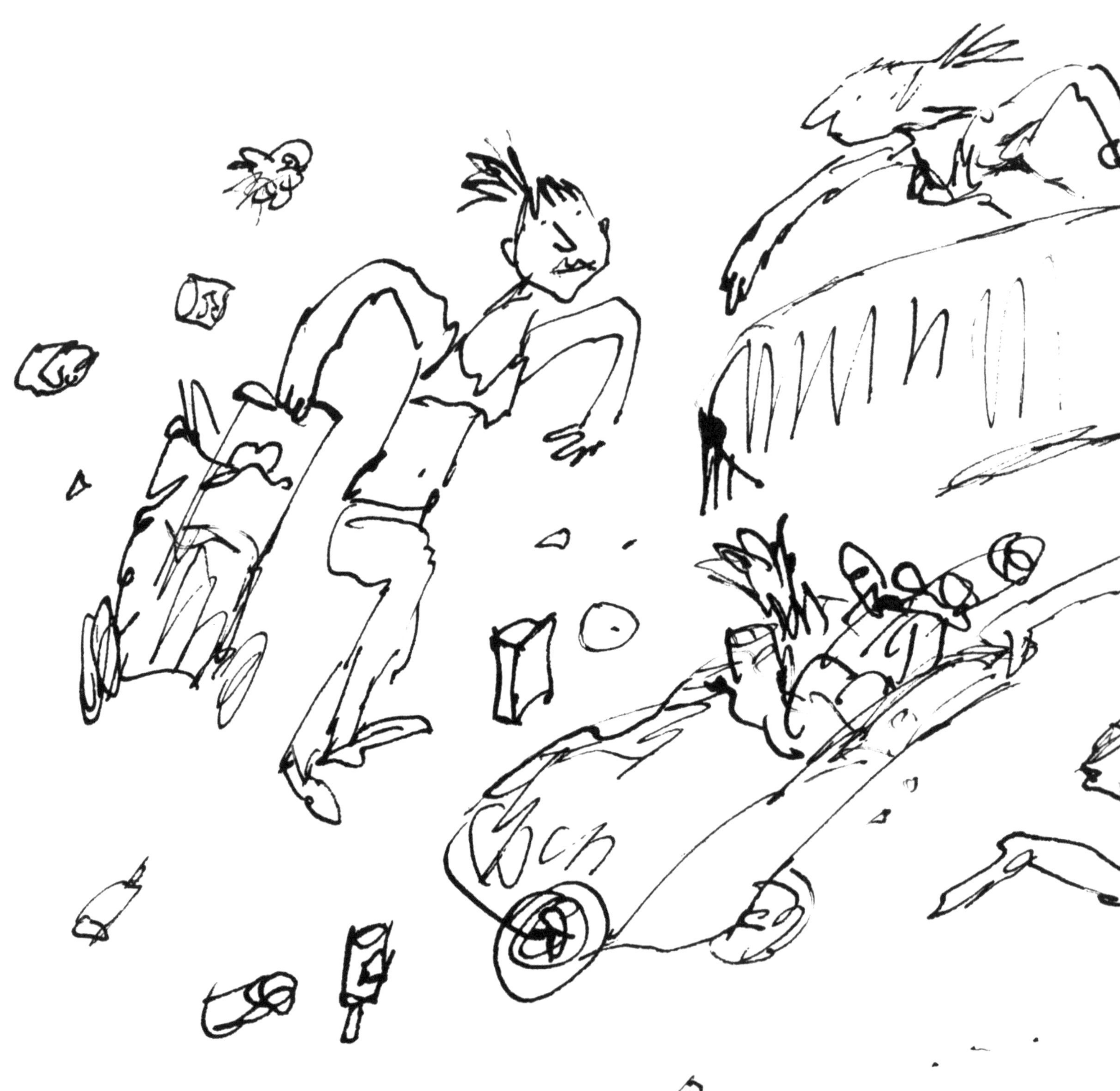

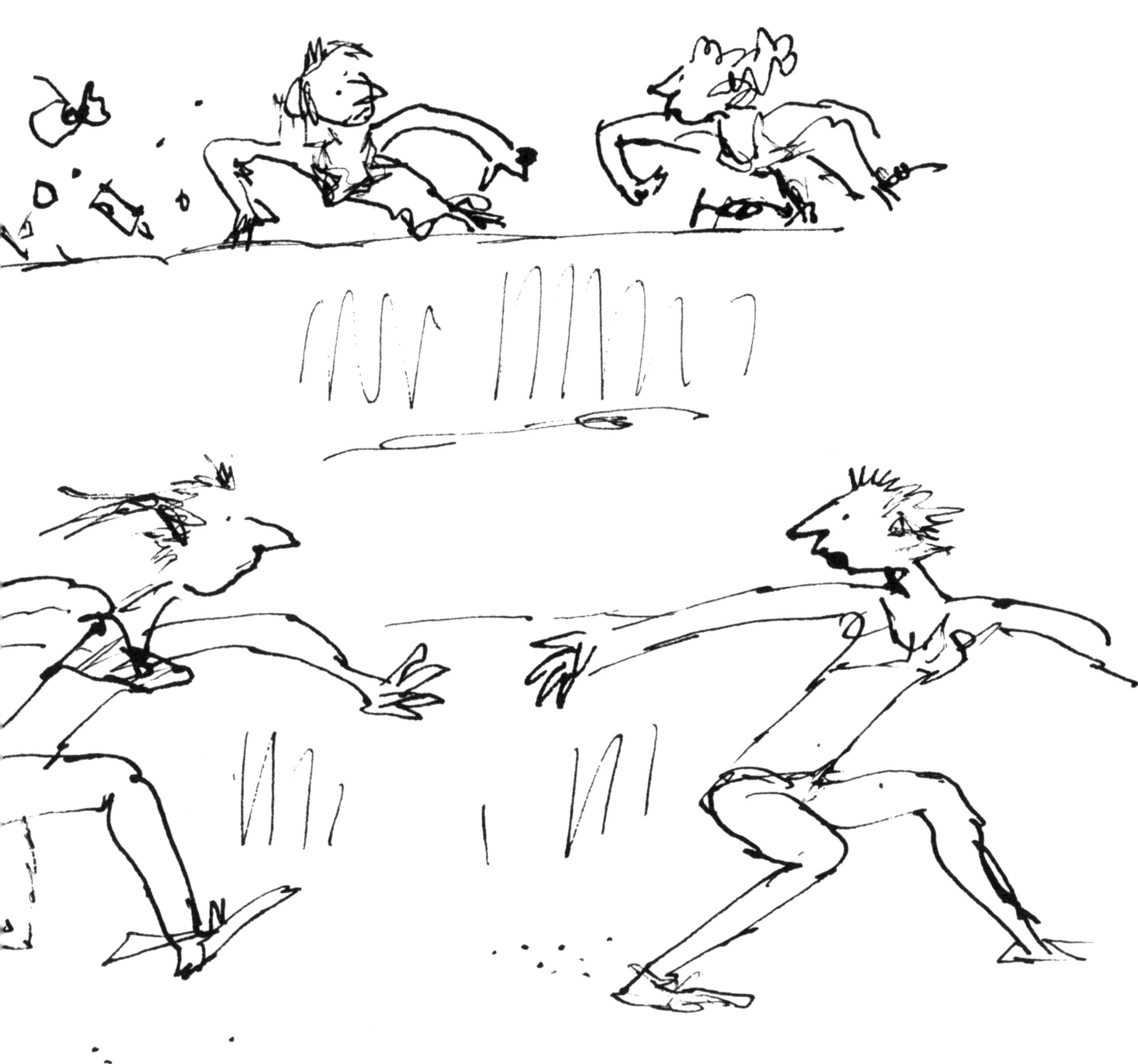

Loaded shopping trolley relay race

High wire and pole vault ice cream cornet event

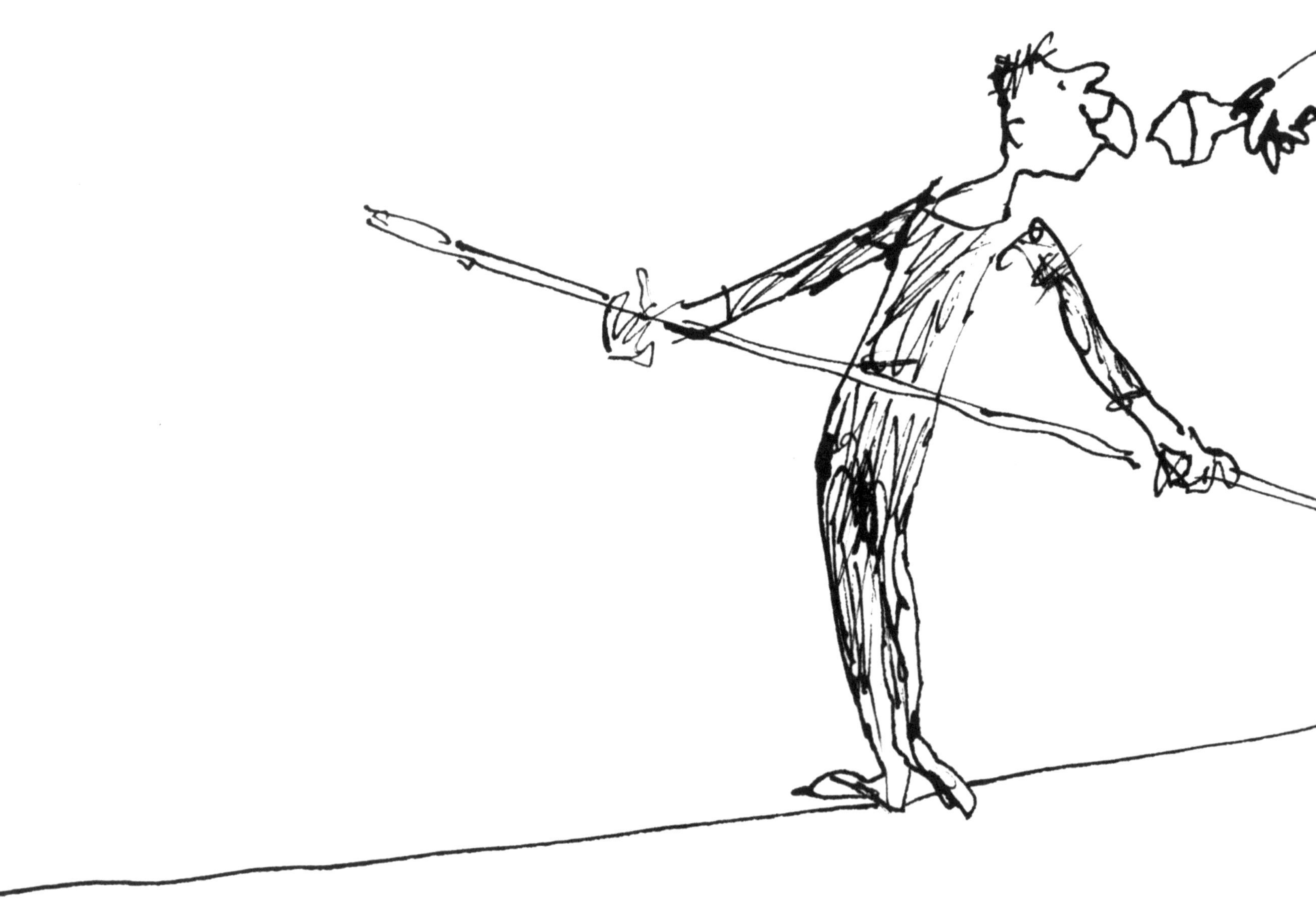

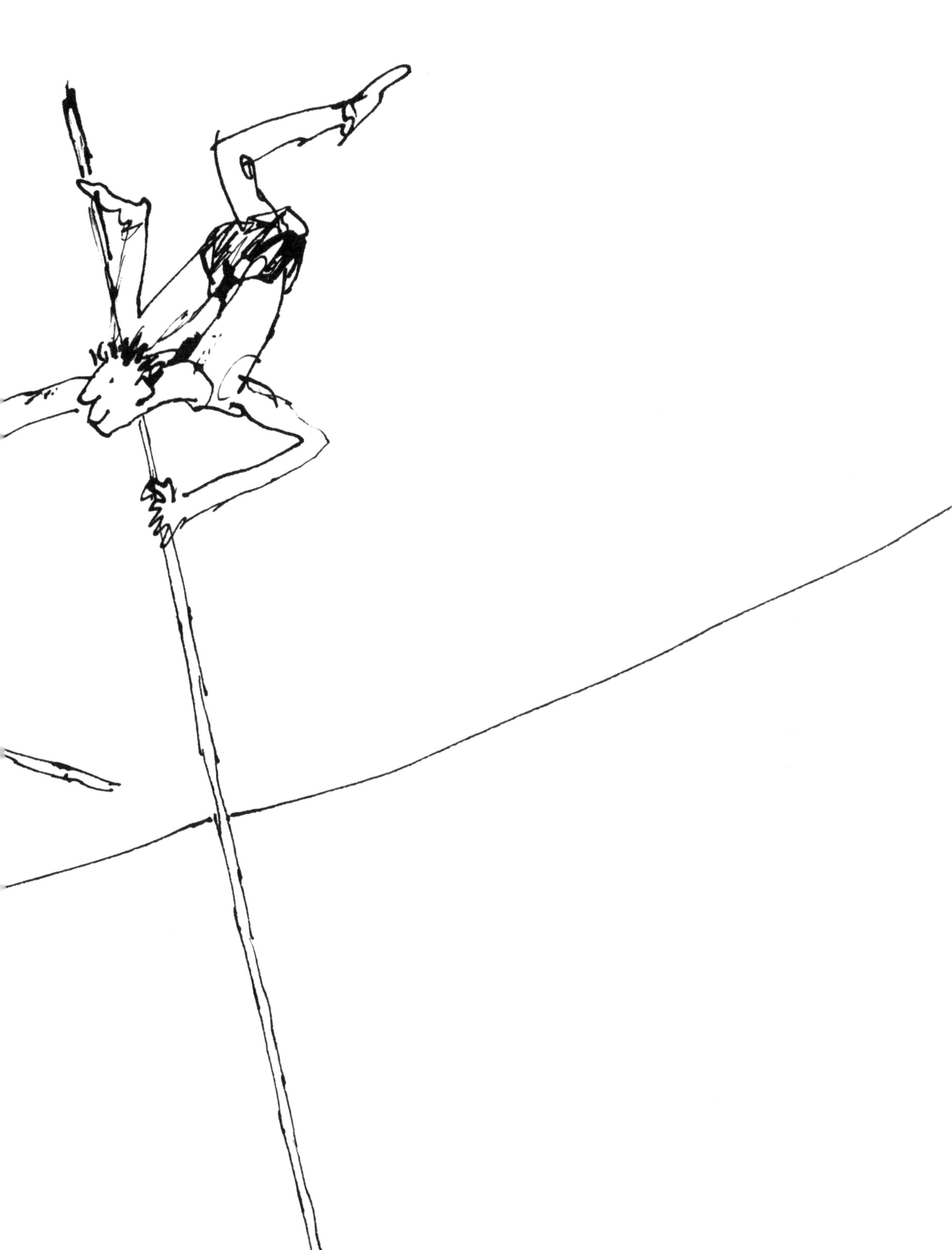

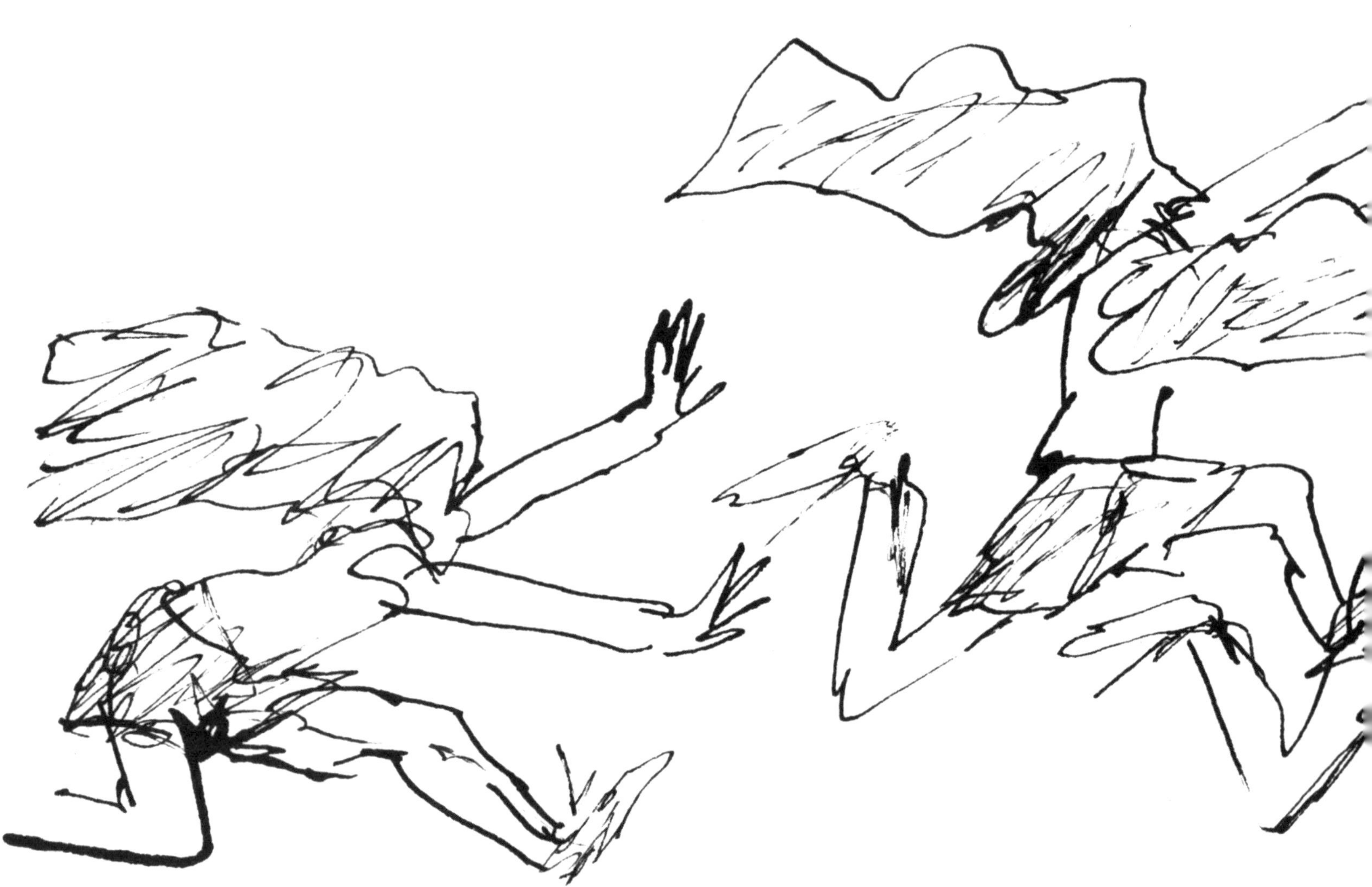

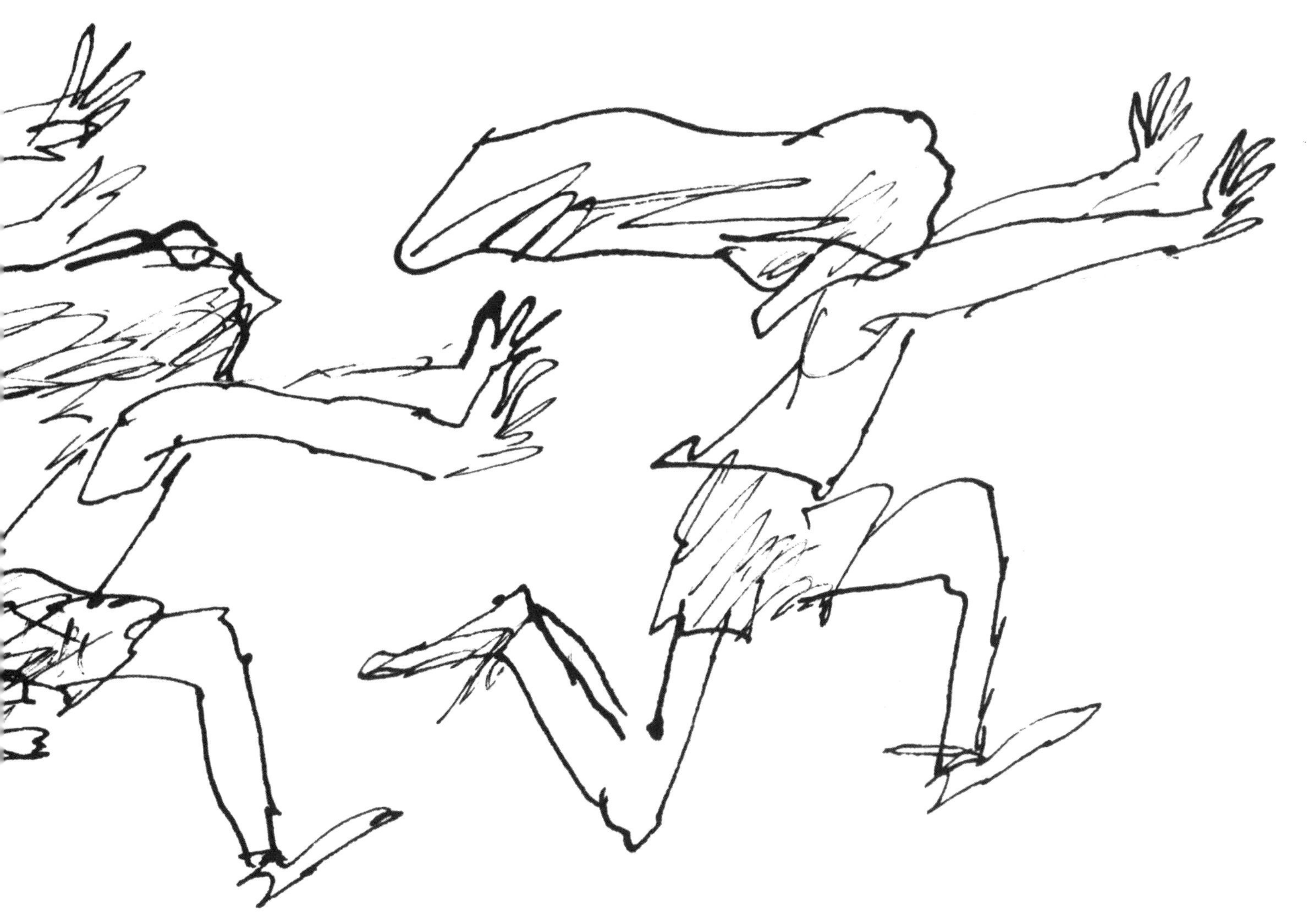

High speed sack race

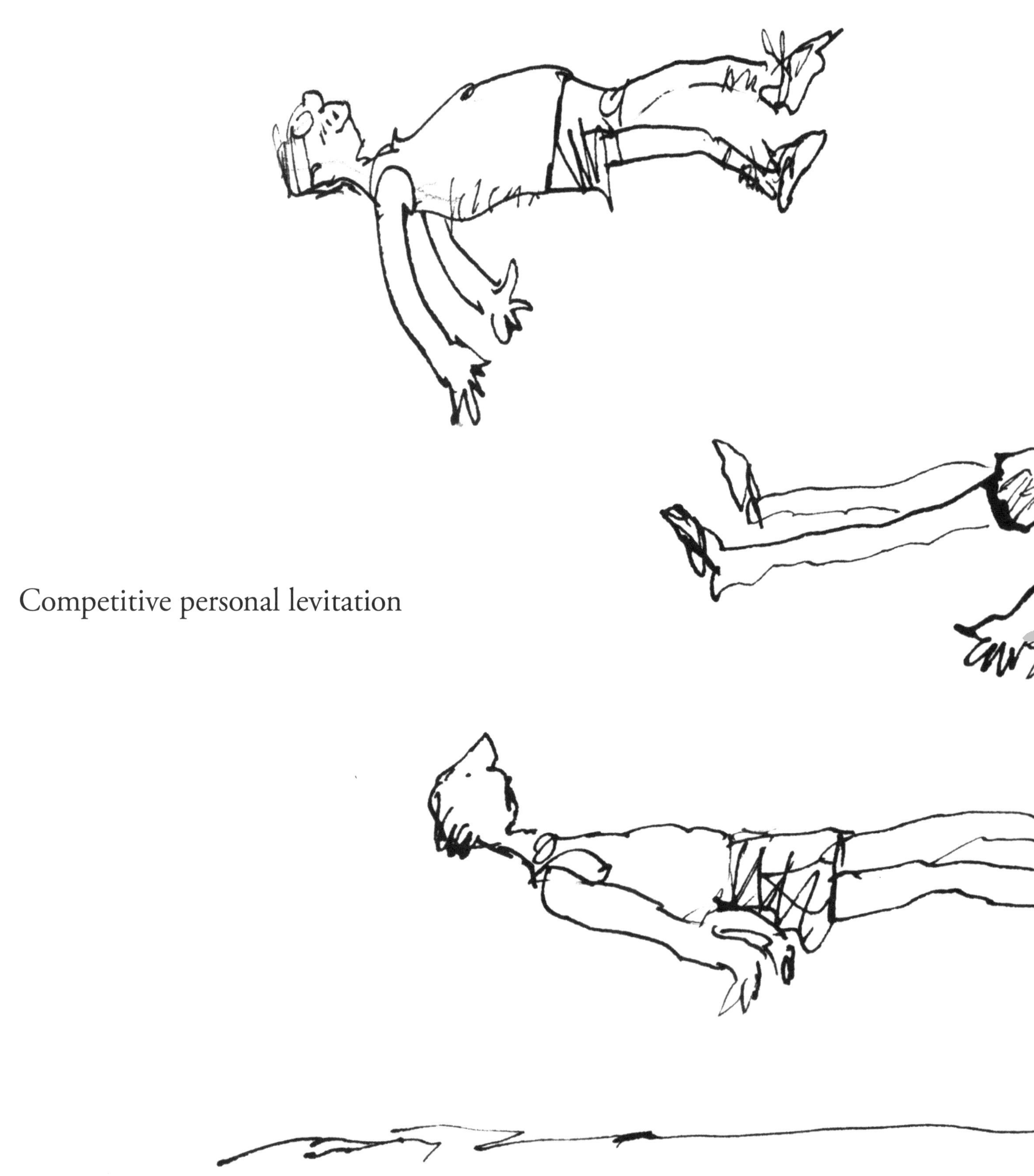

Competitive personal levitation

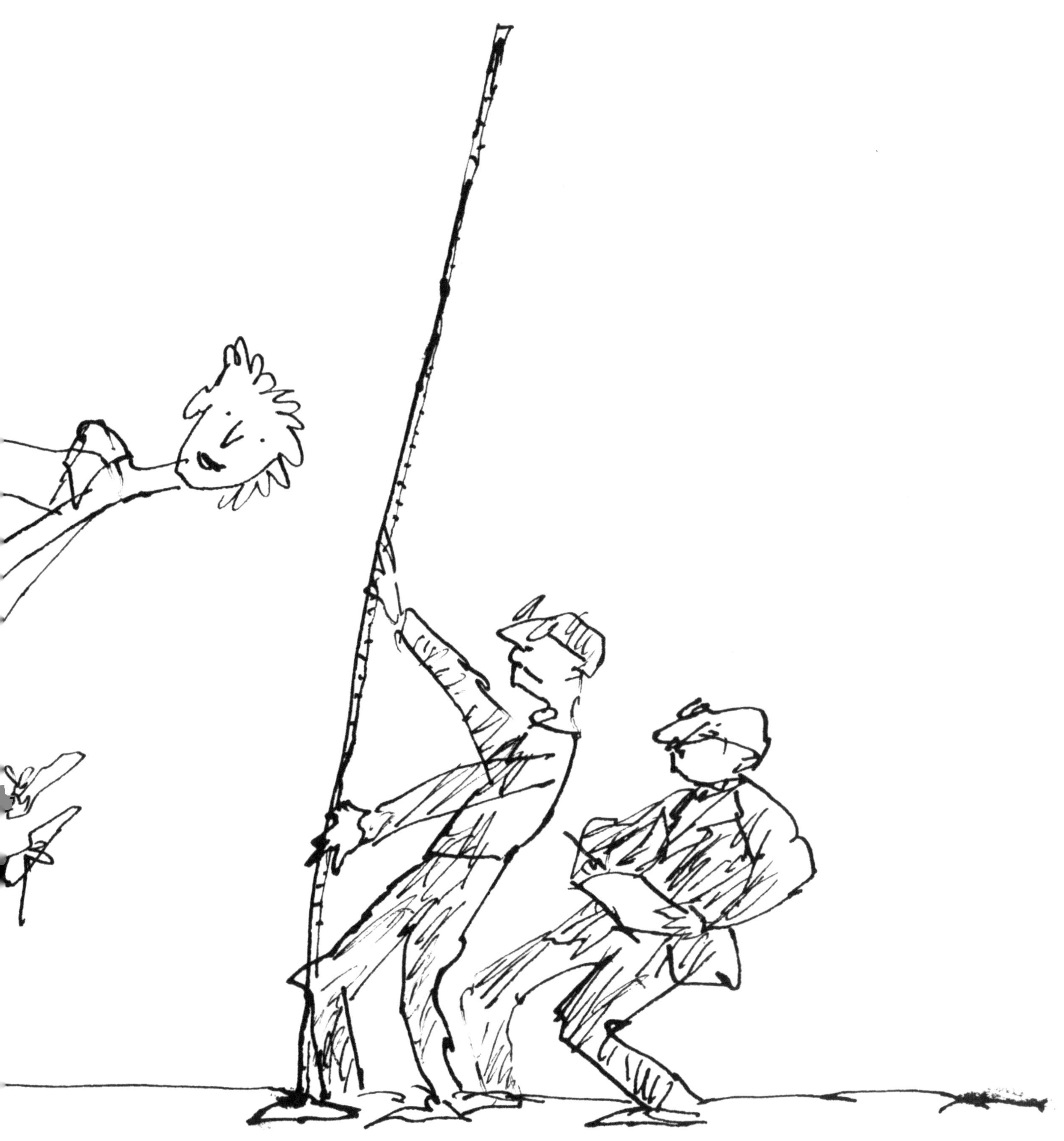

Egg-and-spoon long jump

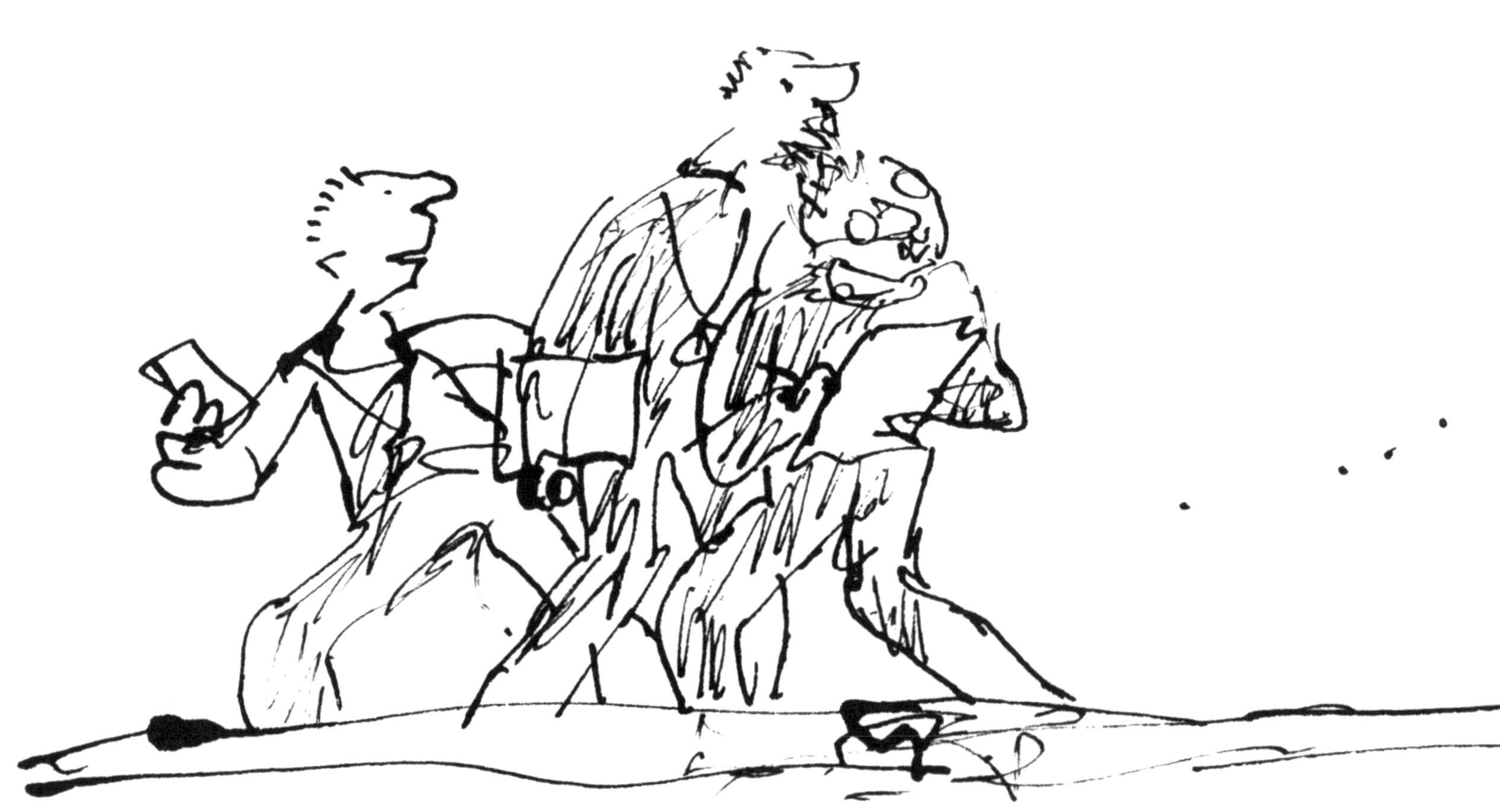

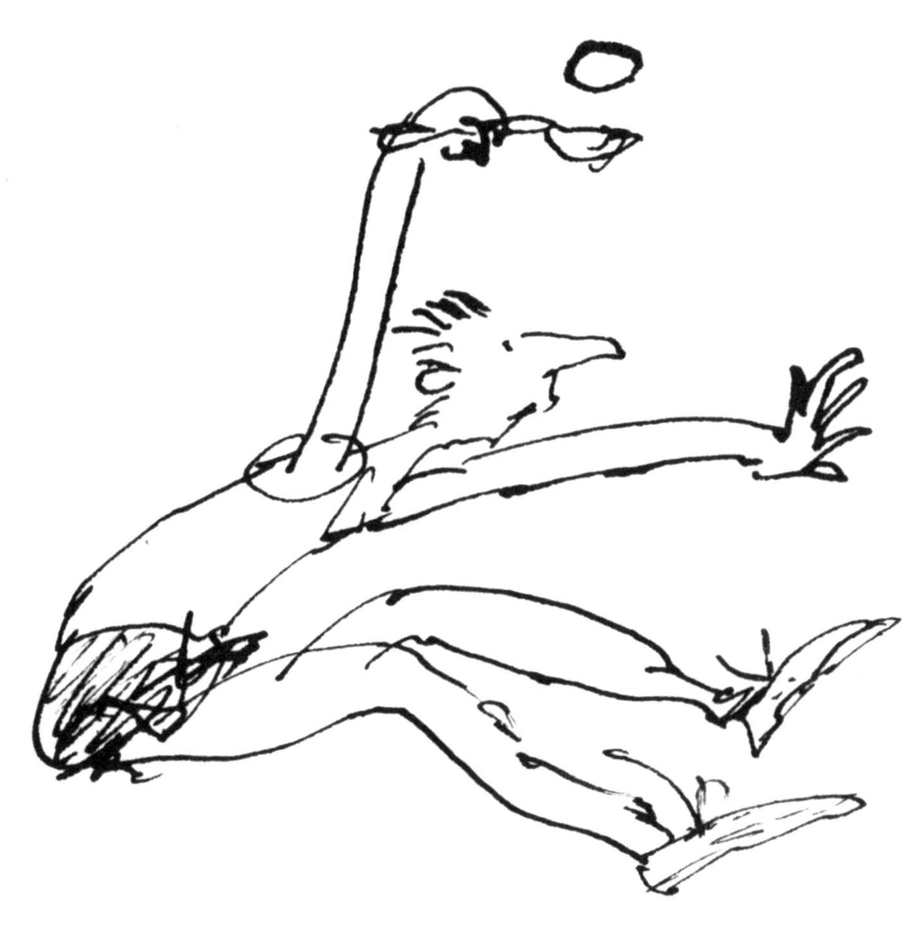

100 metre hand stand race

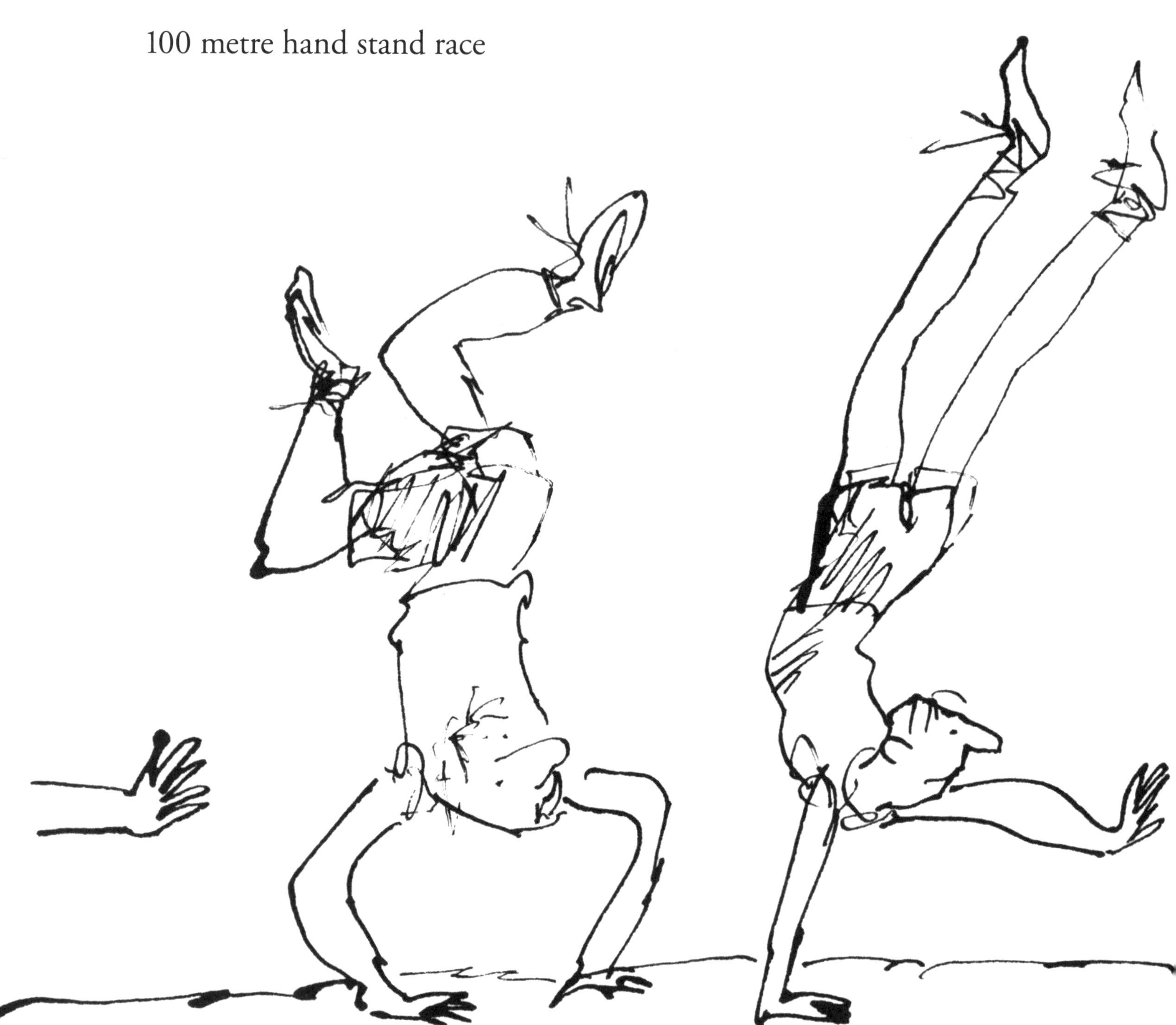

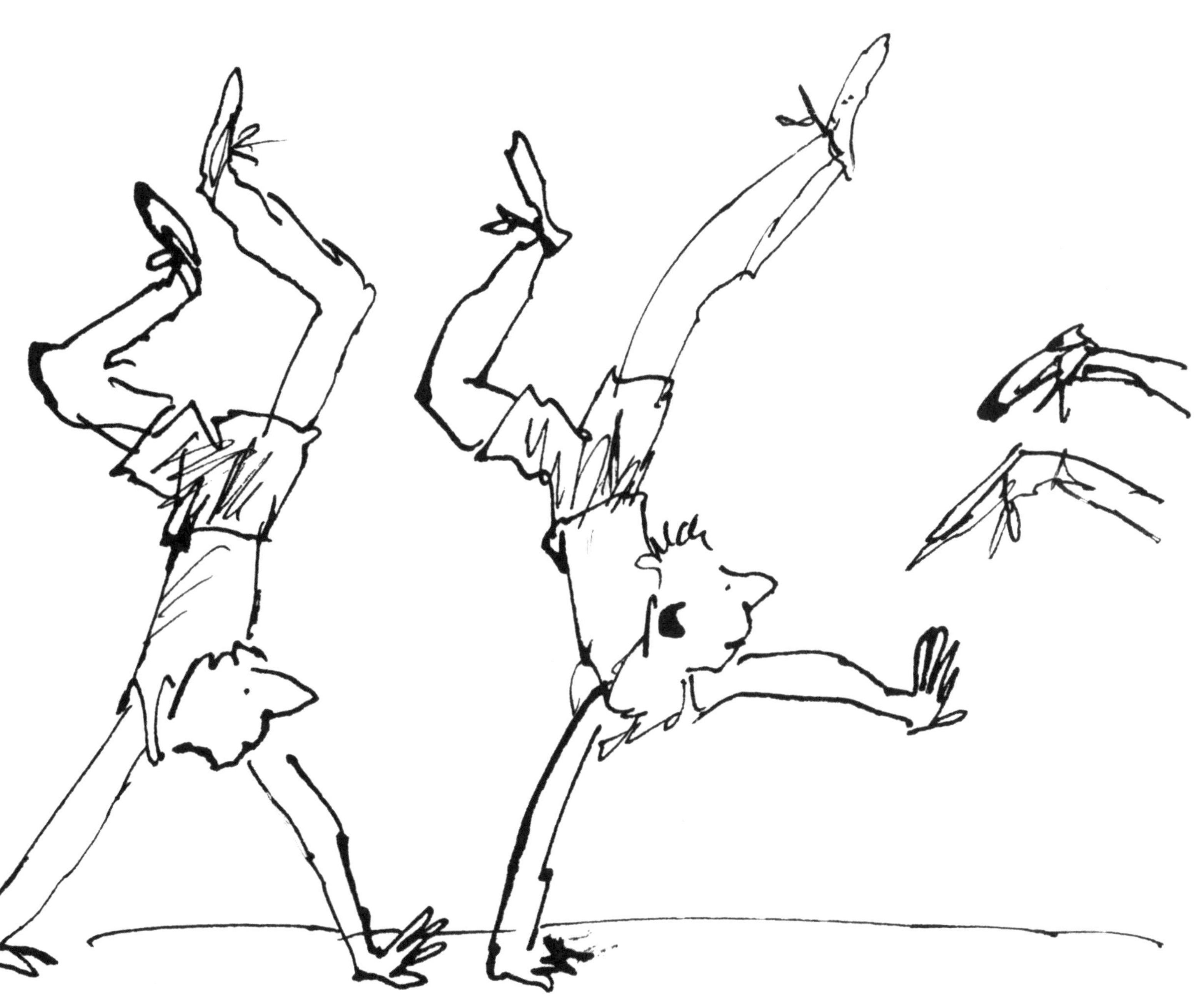

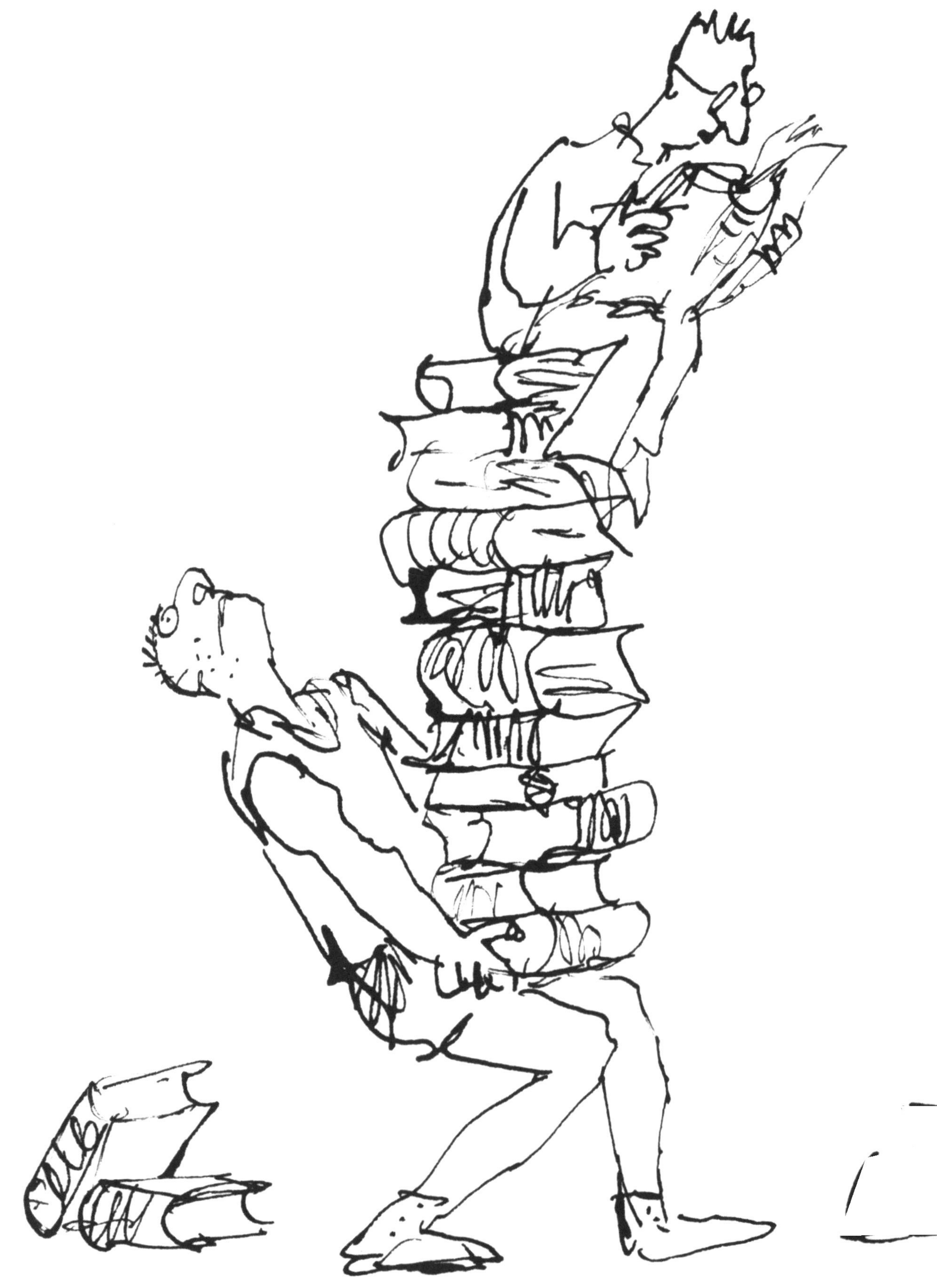

Higher educational weightlifting:
philosophical tomes and a PhD student

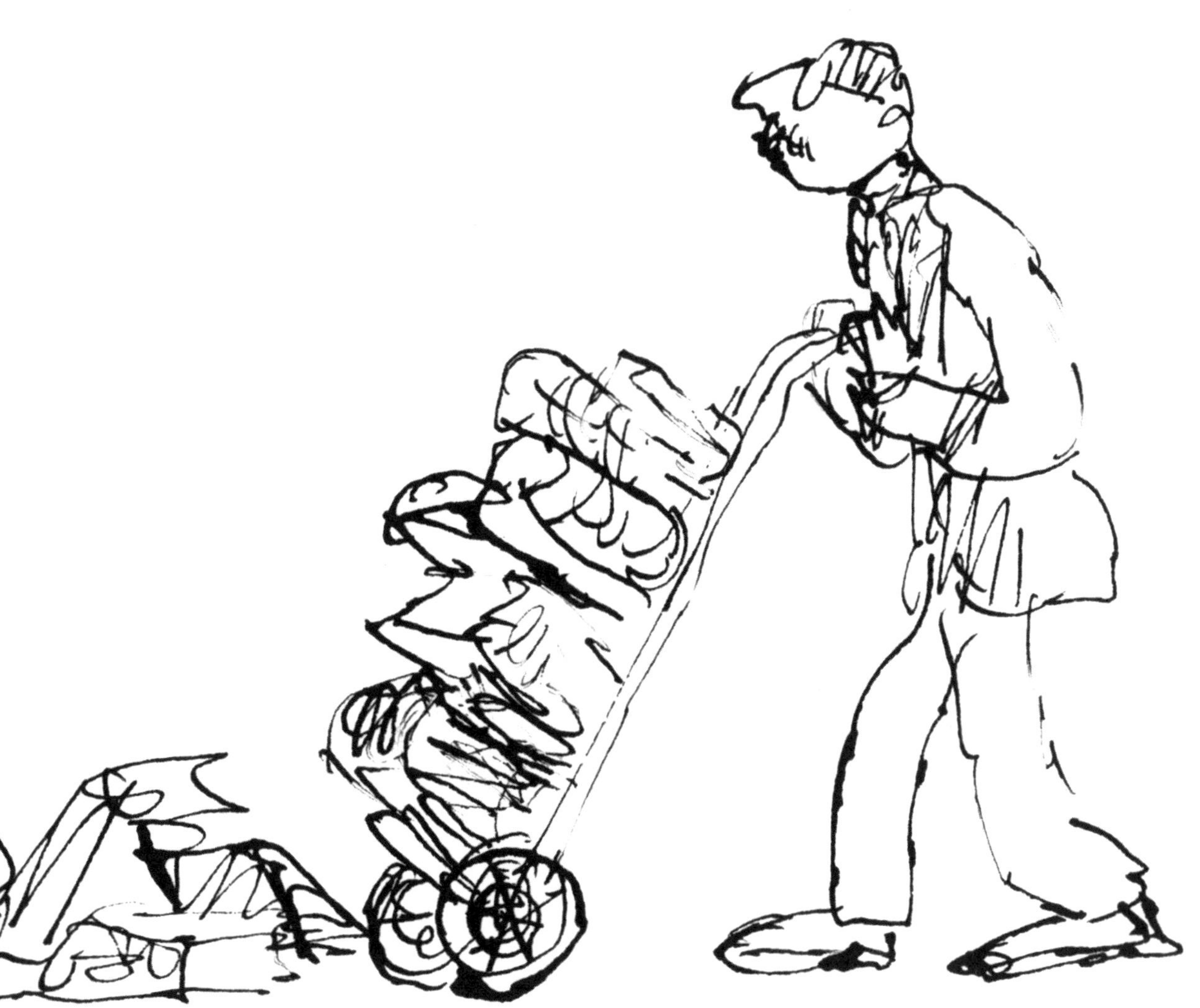

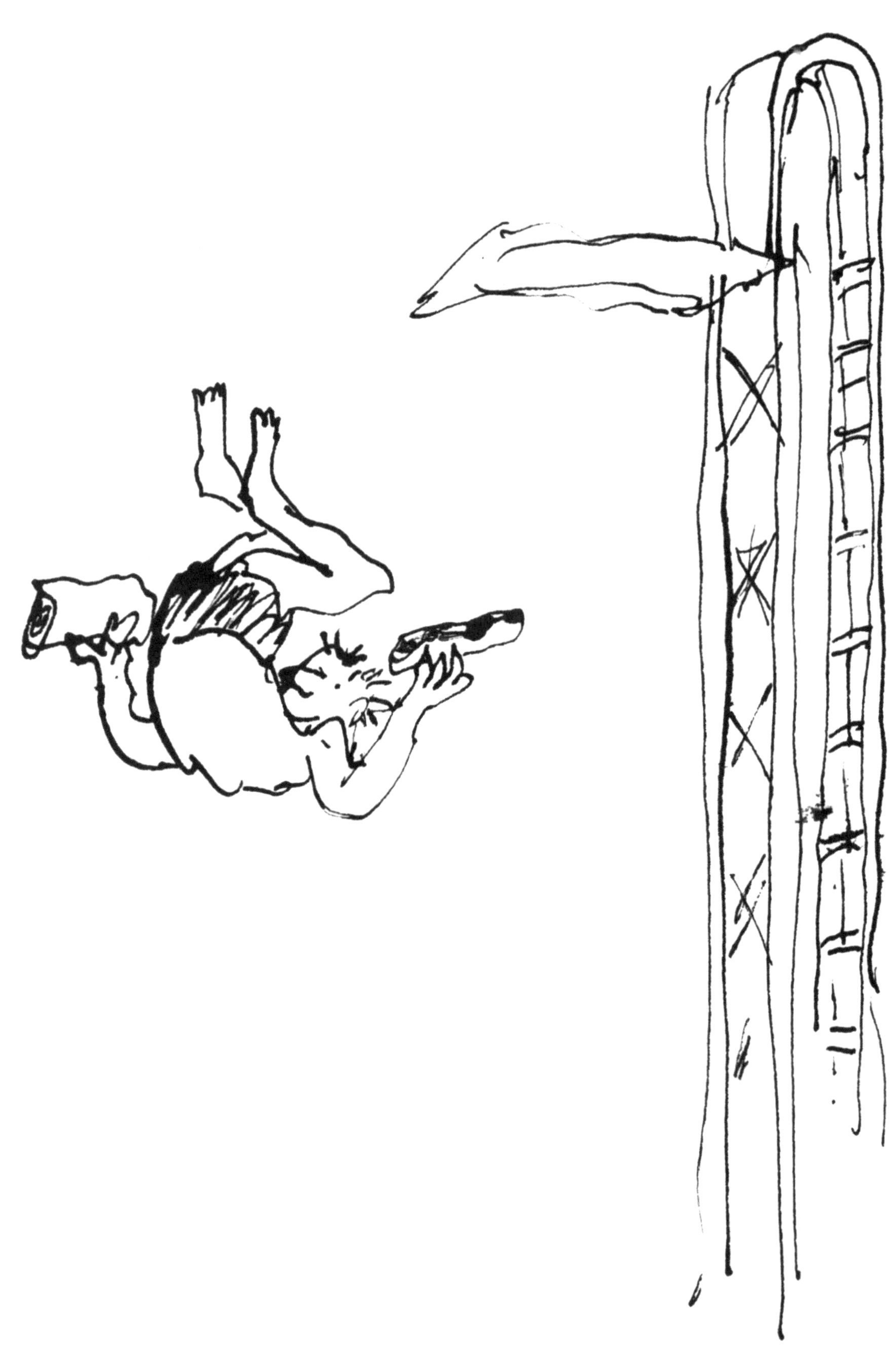

High dive with forward roll,
swiss roll and chocolate eclair

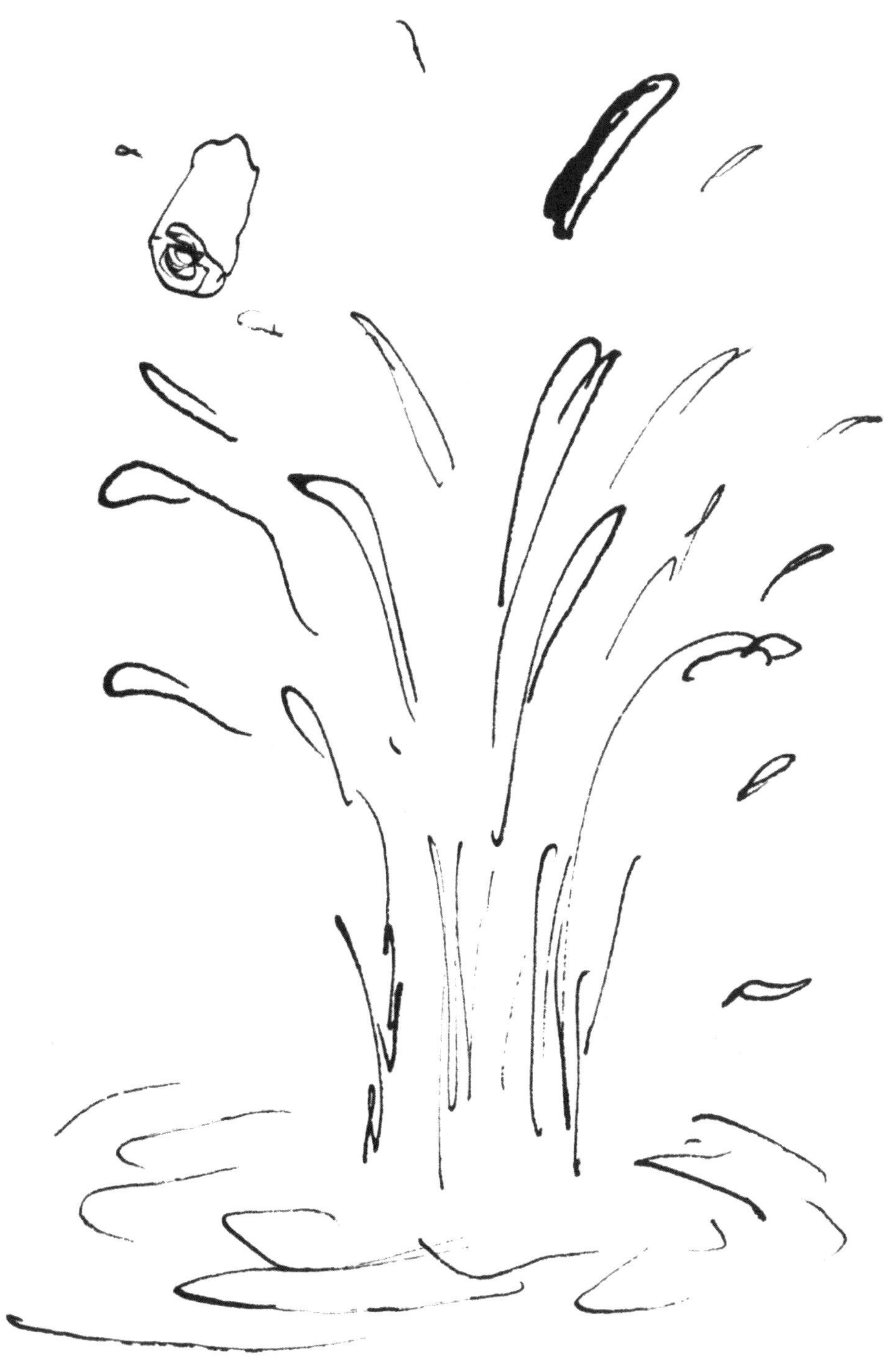

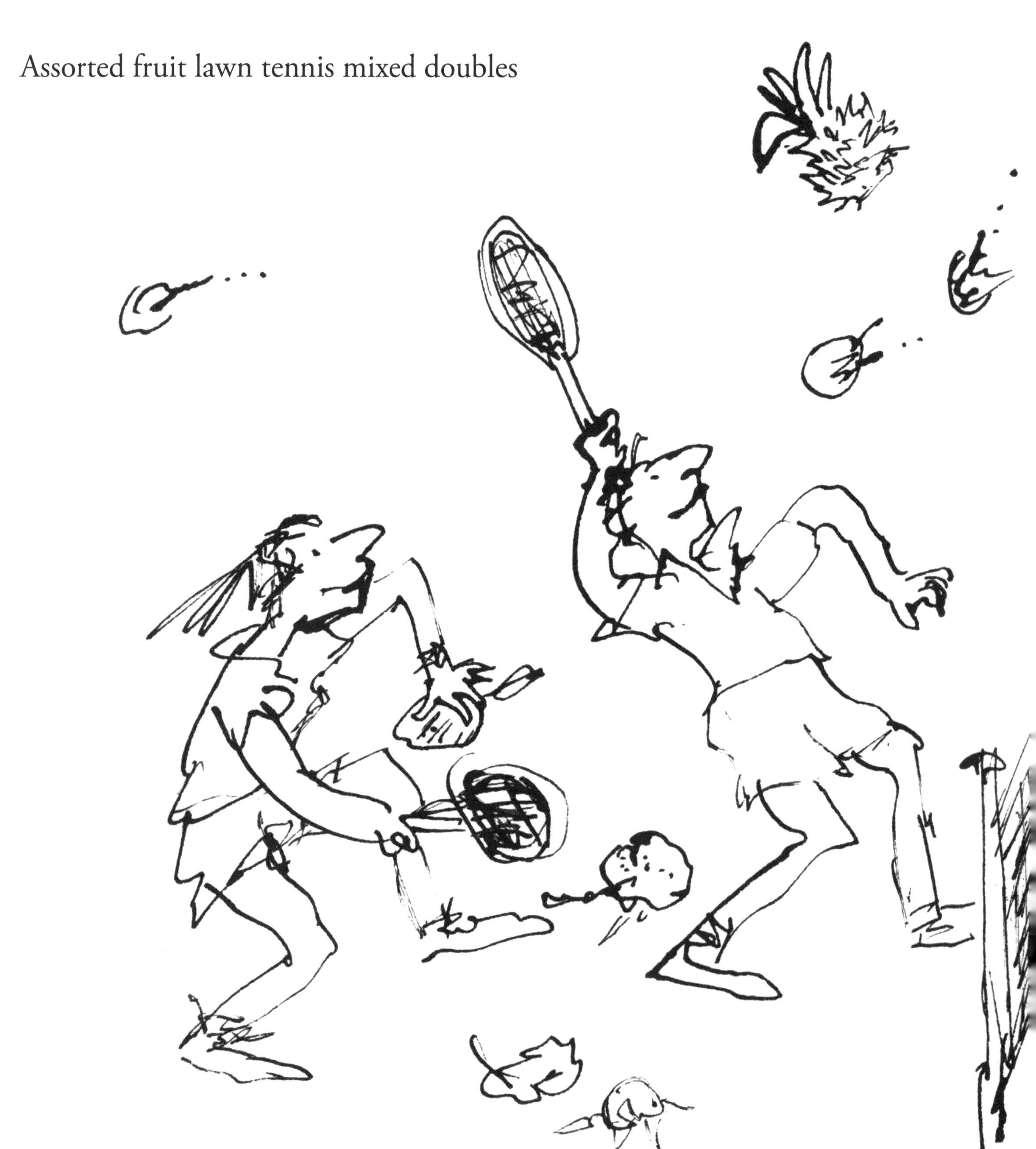

Assorted fruit lawn tennis mixed doubles

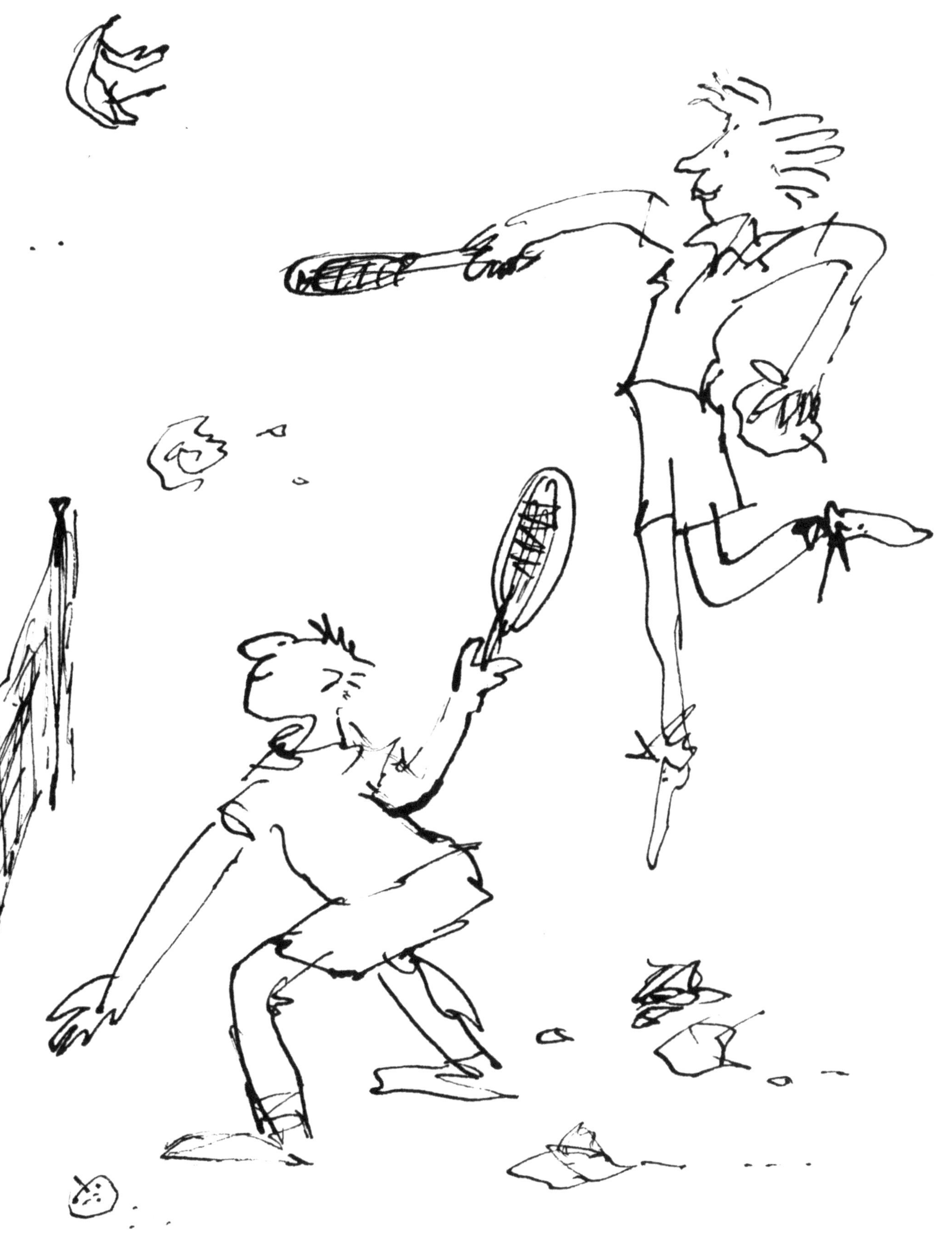

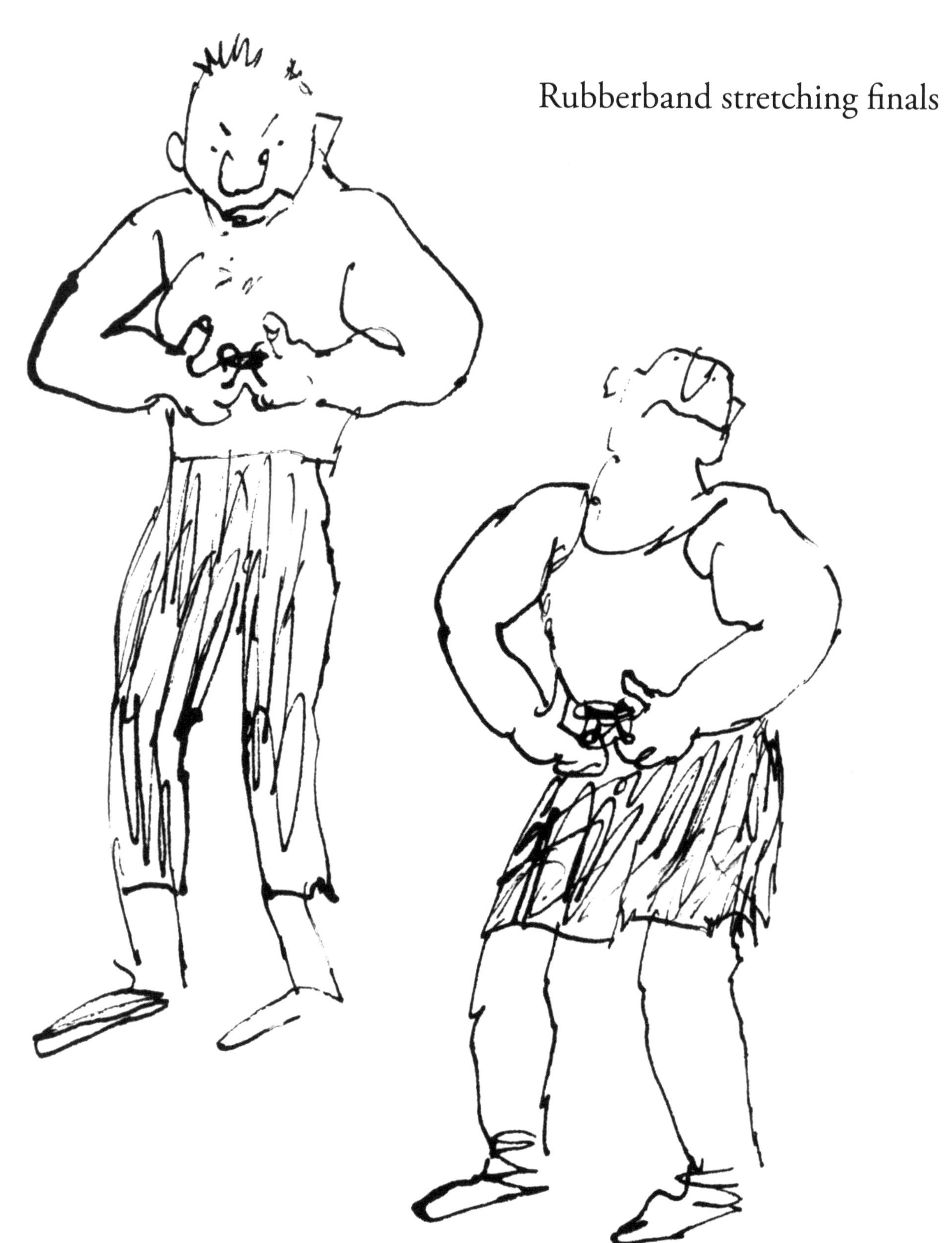

Rubberband stretching finals

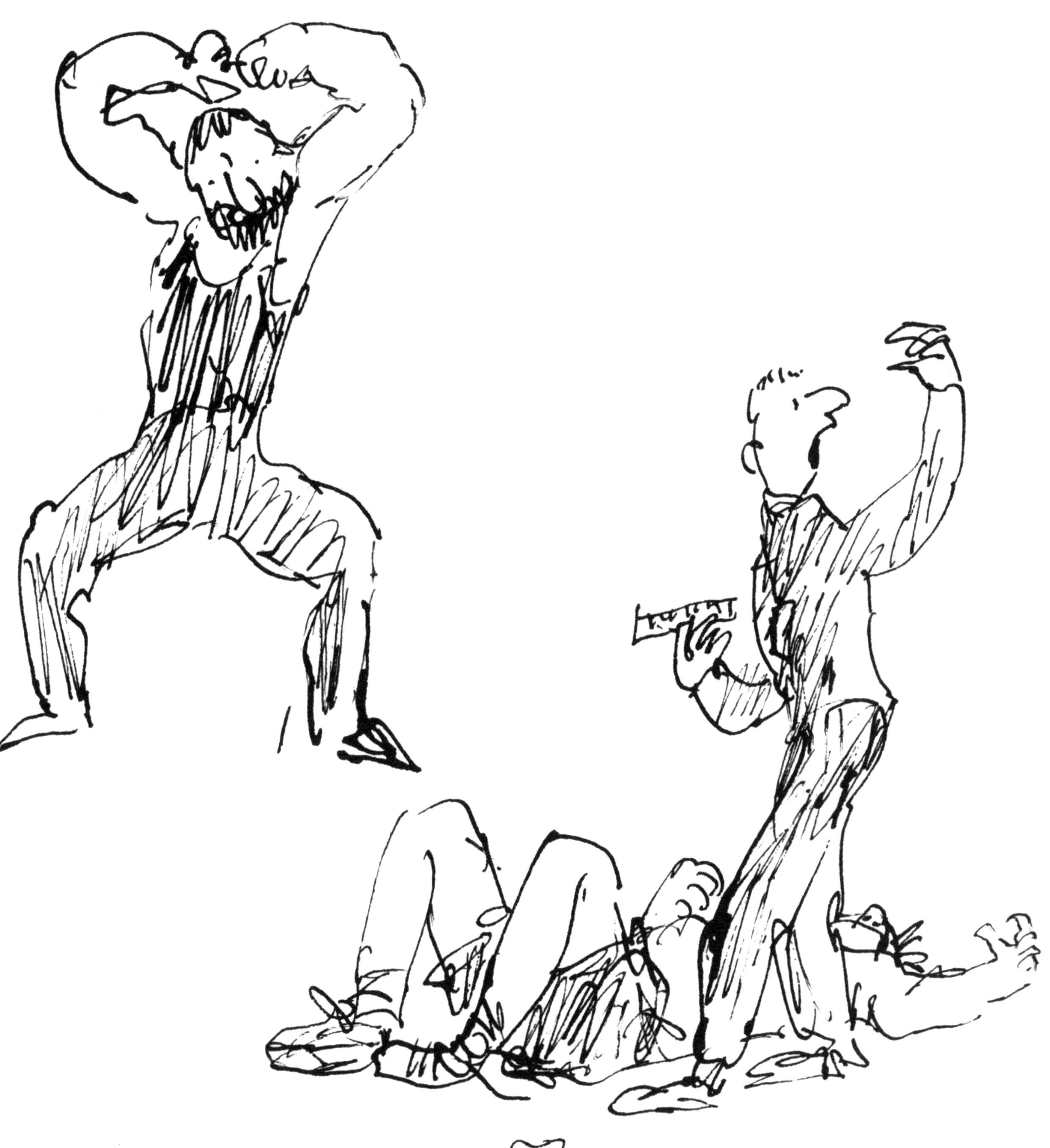

Throwing the luggage

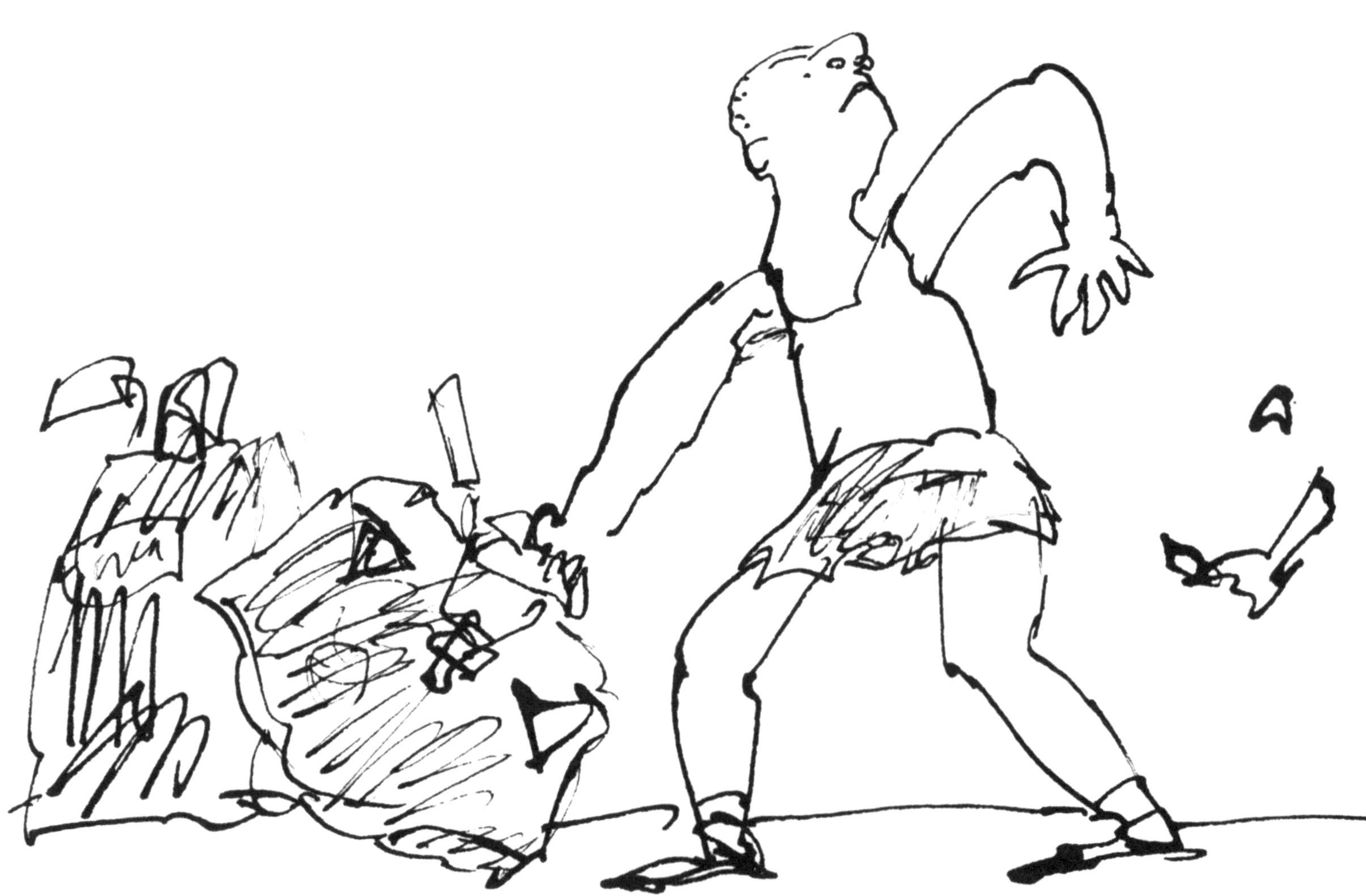

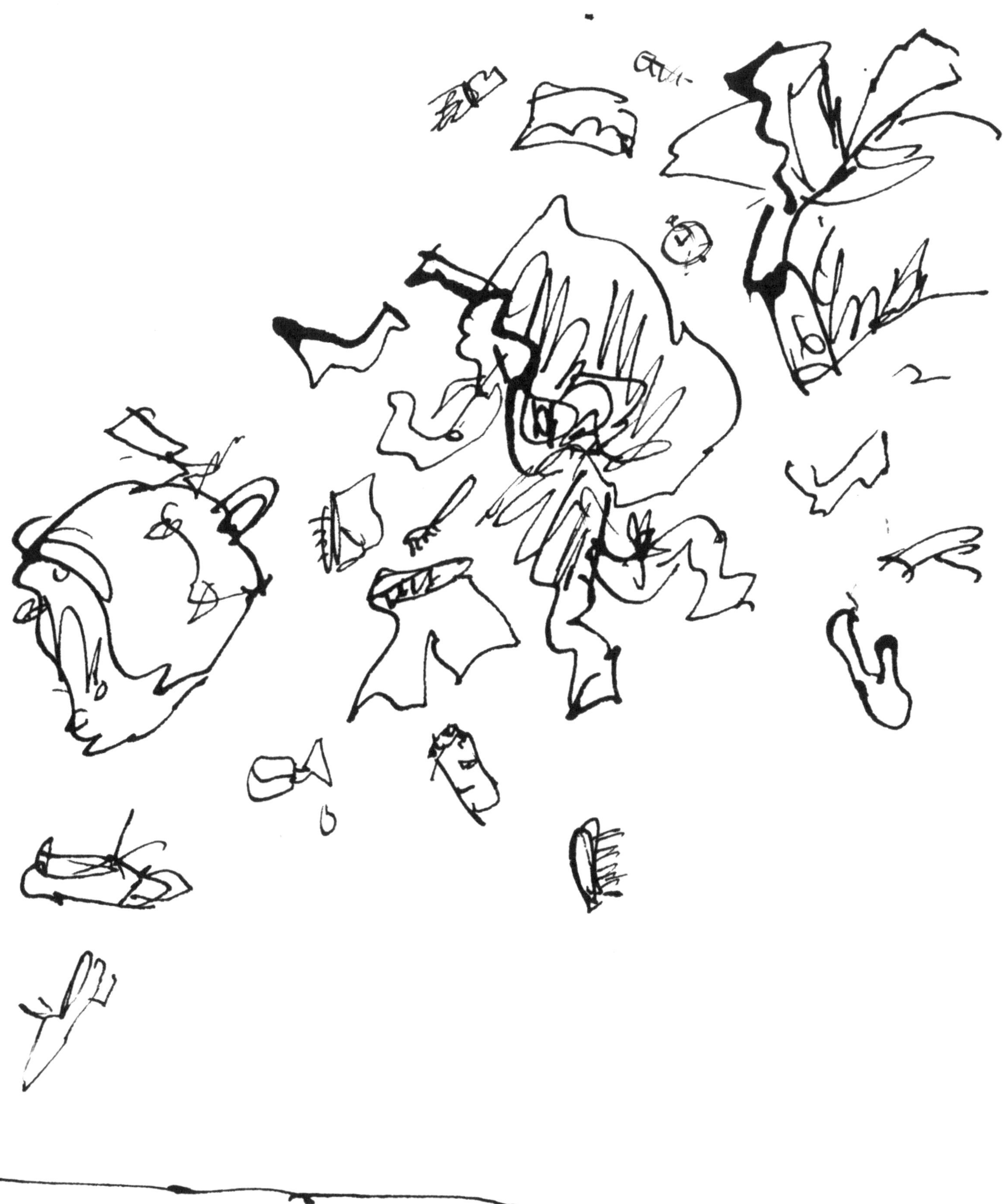

The AB Papers

Other titles:
Constant Readers
The Art of Conversation
Riders by Night
Feet in the Water
A Comfortable Fit
Deliveries from Elsewhere
The Mouse on a Tricycle
Scenes at Twilight
The New Dress

In recent years I have found myself working increasingly in sequences of drawings which explore subjects and techniques which interest me.

These sequences are the origins of *The QB Papers;* they vary in approach and tone, and between reality and fantasy. But I hope that in each of them in its own way will appeal to anyone who likes looking at drawings.

Quentin Blake

The *RB* Papers

Other titles:

Constant Readers

The Art of Conversation

Riders by Night

Feet in the Water

A Comfortable Fit

Deliveries from Elsewhere

The Mouse on a Tricycle

Scenes at Twilight

The New Dress

In recent years I have found myself working increasingly in sequences of drawings which explore subjects and techniques which interest me.

These sequences are the origins of *The QB Papers;* they vary in approach and tone, and between reality and fantasy. But I hope that in each of them in its own way will appeal to anyone who likes looking at drawings.

Quentin Blake